Out There Somewhere

Mick Manning and
Brita Granström

W

FRANKLIN WATTS

NEW YORK • LONDON • SYDNEY

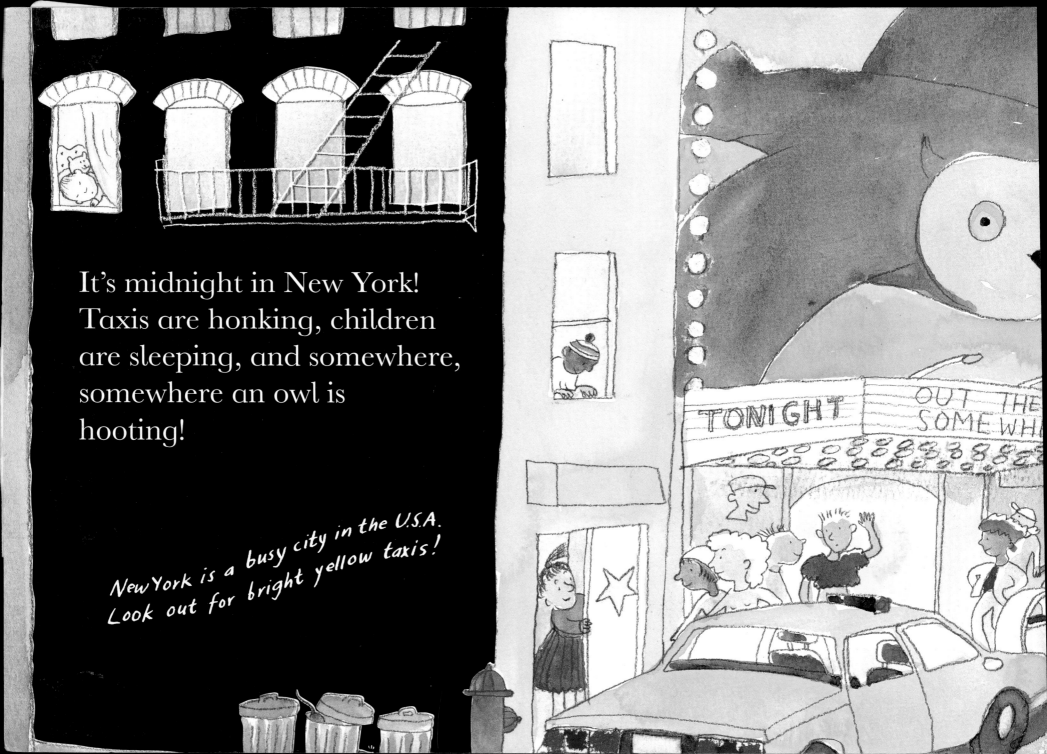

It's midnight in New York!
Taxis are honking, children
are sleeping, and somewhere,
somewhere an owl is
hooting!

New York is a busy city in the U.S.A.
Look out for bright yellow taxis!

TONIGHT   OUT THE
SOME WH

3

It's midnight in New York – but out there somewhere, it's dawn near Newcastle. Most people are still snoring, but the postman is out and about and the cows have already been milked.

Newcastle is a busy town in England, but it is surrounded by farmland.

It's dawn near Newcastle – but out there somewhere it's lunchtime in Taipei. A dragon comes dancing down the street! Look! Three men are doing their exercises. Above the din they can hear a bird calling.

6

Dragon parties are held in cities all over Taiwan.

7

It's lunchtime in Taipei – but out there somewhere it's two in the morning in Brasilia. A little girl has woken up. There's a party going on! She peeps out at the crazy moths dancing around the candles.

Brasilia is a city in Brazil where carnivals and parties can go on all night.

It's two in the morning in Brasilia — but out there somewhere people in Moscow have already eaten breakfast. A car has broken down in the middle of the rush hour! Angry drivers are honk-honking their horns…

Russia has hot summers, but the winters are
icy cold. Moscow is often covered in snow.

11

It's already after breakfast in Moscow
– but out there somewhere it's only
six o'clock in Amsterdam.
A boat chugs along the canal
as joggers come panting and steaming
along the path.

Amsterdam is in Holland—
from here tulips and other
flowers are delivered to
flower shops all over Europe.

13

It's six o'clock in Amsterdam –
but out there somewhere it's midday
near Guilin, in China. Bikes are whizzing
past the paddy fields where wild cranes
are catching frogs. The cranes are
whoop-whoop-whooping!

14

Paddy fields are fields full of water where rice plants grow.

It's midday near Guilin – but out there somewhere it's early afternoon in Tokyo. Electric signs flicker and pulse. People are buying hot dogs, personal stereos are playing tss ss tss…

Tokyo is a very modern city in Japan full of flickering electric signs.

17

It's early afternoon in Tokyo – but out there somewhere it's time for the morning shopping in Madras.
The markets are bustling, crowds are pushing and shoving. Monkeys are stealing bread and fruit.

Indian cities like Madras have markets selling spices, sugary sweets and brightly coloured fabrics.

19

It's shopping time in Madras – but out there somewhere it's breakfast time near Cape Town and the sun is already heating up the roofs. Mums are waving and kissing goodbye. Children rush for the bus swinging their school bags.

Cape Town is a city on the tip
of Africa. It's a good place to
grow grapes and pineapples.

21

It's breakfast time near Cape Town – but out there somewhere it's mid-afternoon on the Gold Coast and "surf's up". In the blink of an eye three skateboarders flip by. Far out in the bay a group of dolphins do somersaults.

The Gold Coast is in Australia – a great place for swimming and surfing.

23

MAX

It's mid-afternoon on the Gold Coast – but out there somewhere dusk is falling near Easter Island. A yacht is bobbing up and down. Mum and Dad are drinking coffee while baby is asleep. Far below them a whale starts to sing...

Easter Island is in the middle of the Pacific Ocean. Can you see the huge stone faces in the background? It's a mystery who carved them!

25

Dusk is falling near Easter Island, but it's dawn near Newcastle and lunchtime in Taipei. It's two in the morning in Brasilia and rush hour in Moscow. It's six o'clock in Amsterdam and midday near Guilin. It's early afternoon in Tokyo and shopping time in Madras. It's breakfast time near Cape Town and mid-afternoon on the Gold Coast…

And it's midnight in New York!

When it's midnight in New York it's all of these times all over the World!

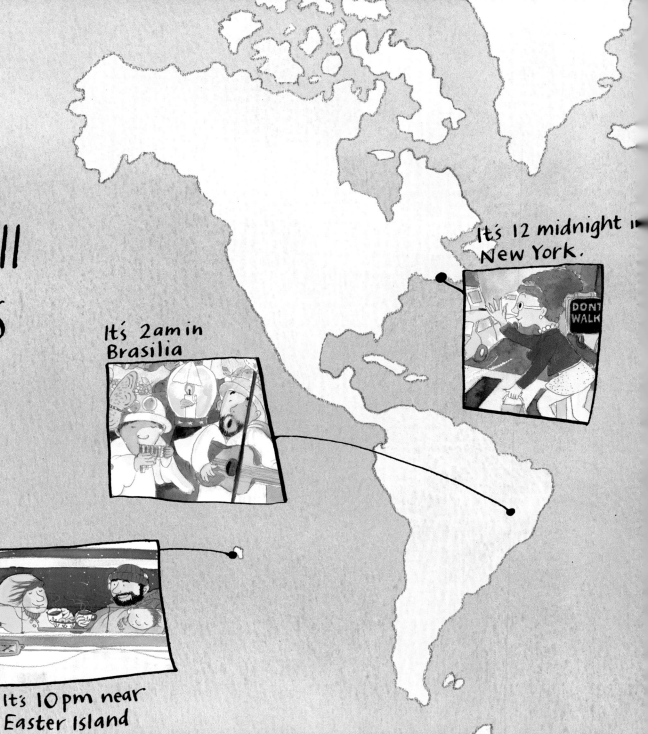

It's 12 midnight in New York.

It's 2am in Brasilia

It's 10pm near Easter Island

It's 5am near Newcastle

It's 8am in Moscow

It's 1pm in Taipei

It's 2pm in Tokyo

It's 6am in Amsterdam

It's 12 midday near Guilin

It's 10.30 am in Madras

It's 3pm on the Gold Coast

It's 7am near Cape Town

29

As the Earth slowly spins one half of the world faces the sun and the other side is in darkness. That's why it's different times in different parts of the world.

Sun

When you are fast asleep in the middle of the night someone else far away is wide awake!

Helpful words

Days There are 24 hours in a day. A day starts from midnight.

Hours An hour is made up of sixty minutes and each minute is made up of sixty seconds.

pm and am All the hours after midnight are called *am* – 1am, 2am and so on until midday. After midday they are called *pm* – 1pm, 2pm and so on until midnight (see pages 28-29).

Time around the world In the past, different countries, and sometimes even cities, had their own system of time. A day could begin at lunchtime, or even sunset! The invention of trains changed all that. It became too complicated to catch a train when each place measured time in a different way. Over a hundred years ago a system of world time was introduced.

Time zones The world is divided into 24 time zones. It is as if lines have been drawn dividing up the world like segments of an orange. These are called timelines. The lines are not always straight, sometimes they curve around countries. This is because it would be too complicated if one part of a country was in a different time zone to the rest. But large countries like the USA are divided into a number of time zones. There is one hour difference as you travel from one time zone to the next.

For Marit and Bosse

First published in 1998 by Franklin Watts,
96 Leonard Street, London EC2A 4XD

Franklin Watts Australia
14 Mars Rd
Lane Cove
NSW 2066

This edition 1999

Text and illustrations © 1998 Mick Manning and Brita Granström

Series editor: Paula Borton
Art director: Robert Walster

A CIP catalogue record is available from the British Library.
Dewey Classification 910

Printed in Singapore
ISBN 0 7496 3037 X (cased); 0 7496 3444 8 (pbk.)